EQUITATION THE
TRUTH

EQUITATION THE TRUTH

Text by
Martin Diggle

Illustrations by
Maggie Raynor

J.A. ALLEN
LONDON

British Library Cataloguing in Publication Data
A catalogue record for this book is available from the
British Library
ISBN 0.85131.583.6

Published in Great Britain in 1993 by
J.A. Allen & Company Limited,
1 Lower Grosvenor Place, Buckingham Palace Road,
London, SW1W OEL.

CONTENTS

CONTENTS

Author's Note

The characters mentioned by name in this book are entirely real; any similarity to fictional characters is purely coincidental.

I have assured the publisher that none of those named herein will attempt libel action, for the following reasons:

1. Since they are friends of mine, they are aware that I have no money.

2. Knowing me as they do, they will recognise that, even if I did have money, I would rather go to prison than pay any of them a penny piece.

3. They will be aware that what is written about them is quintessentially true, and generally understated. Furthermore, being the sort of people they are, they are more likely to glory in their moments of public notoriety than to consult legal advisers.

Martin Diggle.
Somewhere in South America.
Undated.

ILLUSTRATOR'S NOTE

ALL THE ILLUSTRATIONS IN THIS BOOK are copied from photographs of the author's friends. I only did it for the money.

Maggie Raynor.

SOME OF THE AUTHOR'S FRIENDS.

INTRODUCTION

LOOK, I KNOW THAT INTRODUCTIONS CAN be boring, but I really think you should read this one, because I don't want you to buy this book under a misapprehension. (The publisher wouldn't mind *what* you bought it under — except, of course, the market price — but then publishers tend to let financial considerations cloud their altruistic sensibilities.) The thing is, there are a lot of horse books about with very grand titles: *How To Ride More Grand National Winners*; *Score Tens At Dressage*; *Olympic Medals On A Plate*; *Be An Equine Genius* and so on.

And what happens? You pay loads of money for them; you study the spectacular photo sequences: 'The author negotiating the lake complex at Badminton whilst riding a series of pirouettes'; you boggle at the diagrams of equine locomotion which look as if they have escaped from a treatise on structural engineering; you read the inspirational text: 'It was a struggle in the early days — daddy had to pawn the butler to buy me my first stable complex'. Then, fired with enthusiasm, you go off to show the world that there is a new equestrian star in the firmament. And you're still rubbish.

Now, I could not sleep easily if I thought that people were buying a book called *Equitation — The Truth* on the assumption that it was a distillation of pure knowledge which would enable the reader to perform feats of unparalleled equestrian virtuosity. The reason I could not do so has little to do with guilt (after all, I'm on a promise of royalties); it is, rather, rooted in a knowledge of horse people drawn from my own circle of friends. As far as the majority are concerned, the idea that there is any power in Heaven or Earth which could produce such an effect is too ridiculous for words and, if they started to believe in such a concept, I would be too worried about all the crazies out there to sleep soundly.

'Hah!', you say. 'Here I am, skulking in a trade stand out of the weather, wondering whether this rather cheap book would make a better Christmas present than yet another grooming kit, and I get insulted in the first minute's reading. Just because this totally obscure author has friends who can't ride, he tars the rest of us with the same brush. I am deeply offended, and shall put this book down and flick through *Score Tens At Dressage*'. Hang on pal. You don't fool me. Too much attitude and a suspiciously new waxed jacket — that's your problem. If you *were* any good at riding, you'd be out there in the pouring rain winning the Power and Speed class or, alternatively, sitting in luxury writing *World Domination On Horseback — An Autobiography*. But you're not.

Anyway, don't take umbrage. Remember, the whole purpose of this introduction is to convince my readership that I'm not conning them. You see, the truth in the title is not the 'truth' as understood by those promoting Asiatic cults, tabloid journalists or politicians; it is the truth as in real life. All the anecdotes herein recall events which really happened, and a worryingly large proportion of the verses were inspired by events which really happened. This is a book which acknowledges that people score *fours* at dressage — and that only on a good day, when the judge has a pretty writer who is sending unmistakeable signals of devotion with her free hand. Moreover, this is a book which understands that people *like* scoring fours at dressage, because it gives so much scope for (albeit, not likelihood of) improvement; a book which realises that Hell is a place where you find yourself on a perfect horse, ride a Grand Prix Special scoring those infernal tens for everything then, when you ask

'What next?' are told 'The same again...for ever'.

So, what are my qualifications for writing this book? Twenty years of real-life riding: twenty years of torn breeches, sore bits, strained bits, mud, ignominy, worry, heartache and penury. The realisation that riding is, these days, simply a more socially acceptable (if more expensive) form of self abuse than being a flagellant friar...

I don't know though. Would it be currently more socially acceptable to walk through Leicester Square in full riding gear or in sackcloth, with a cat o' nine tails? A nice point. I know, you read this book (*buy it* first), and I'll see if I can come up with a rude habit.

THE MASTERS EXPLORE THE TRUTH.

The Making of a Book

Although it may not be apparent from the vacuous, formless ramblings of this book*, I occasionally do some editing work for my publishers. This has given me an insight of what is involved in the production of an equestrian book. The following is a more or less accurate description of the processes concerned:

The equestrian author has had a GREAT THOUGHT
And he bounds out of bed quite convinced that he ought
To essay a new book which expounds a GREAT TRUTH
Which he's sure — had it dawned on him back in his youth —
Would have led to his having become a GREAT MASTER
Whose horses moved lighter, jumped higher, ran faster
Than Klimke's or Sloothaak's or Piggott's or Todd's
Or those other equestrian centaur-like gods.

The equestrian author takes paper and pen
And writes with great haste, pausing just now and then
To insert punctuation in arbitrary; — fashion;!
*And add some italics to indicate **passion**.*
To fuel inspiration and keep at full throttle
He's frequent recourse to a dwindling bottle
And — neat correlation — the redder his nose
As he's warmed to his task, so the purpler the prose.

* As nowhere in this book can we locate the grovelling thanks due to us for publishing these ramblings, there will certainly not be any more. Pub.

5

The equestrian publisher wears a deep frown;
His blood pressure's up, but his sales are down.
Reviews of new works from his house are all dismal
His authors are crass, and their output abysmal.
He needs a new writer so desperate for fame
That a total rehash can be launched in his name...
Then a manuscript, dog-eared and reeking of brandy
Arrives on his desk, and he thinks 'This is handy'.

As he flicks through the pages, he says 'This is grand
It just needs the deft touch of an editor's hand
To cut through the rubbish (perhaps ninety per cent)
And thus unlock the essence of just what is **meant**.
And so staff are let loose with some scissors and paste
And they savage the work with great violence and haste
There is tippexing, snipping, insertion, rewriting
And house style disputes which are settled by fighting.

And so it transpires that The New Equitation
(As the work is now titled) is launched on the nation
And critics write 'fearless' and 'brazen' and 'bold'
And in days the entire first edition is sold.
But what has engendered these sales may be
Not the rather bland text, but the photos (page three)
Supplied by a library which — one must conclude —
Has misheard the title, and thought it read 'Nude'.

Those who are disposed to read on will discover the truth
of this.

6

'I don't care what you've been reading, you're
improperly dressed. Please go home and put on a BHS
approved helmet.'

Pleasure

Crashing through the cattle-crush
Landing in the mire
Riding across country
Is my heart's desire.

Smashing through the sheep pen
Hurtling into space
Whenever I go riding
A smile is on my face.

Lurching through the log pile
Tumbling into gorse
All my greatest pleasures are
Provided by the horse.

'I'M GETTING PLENTY OF HEIGHT — I JUST NEED A LITTLE
MORE BASCULE.'

You Can Lead a Horse to Water

Some years ago, I enjoyed a couple of excellent riding holidays on Dartmoor, staying with a group of friends at a farm near Haytor. The farm was run by a couple named Rosie and Bob, who had several claims to fame. Firstly, they grew, on their muck heap, by far the best marrows I have ever tasted. Secondly, they owned a Collie of impeccable pedigree who would not go near a sheep, and a Pekinese who would have won *One Man and His Dog*. Thirdly, they had a coloured cob named Beau Bob who would spend his time looking for anything vaguely resembling an obstacle, and then make a substantial and determined detour in order to cart his rider over it. Fourthly, Bob himself was on excellent terms with all the innkeepers within riding distance and apparently had accounts with them, since he regularly and generously procured drinks for his guests without ever being seen to hand over any cash.

Outings with Bob were always adventurous and, one day, returning from a long ride over the moor, we came through Widecombe on the day of the fair. This time-honoured event has a considerable equestrian element, and we stopped to watch some showjumping and pony racing; the latter wall-of-death style round a tight, pear-shaped track. It soon became quite obvious that everyone at the fair — with the certain inclusion of the commentator — was gloriously and happily drunk and, when we sampled the scrumpy tent, we realised why. After a while, the cider-inspired Bob suggested that we turn the ride home into a

mounted pub crawl though, in honesty, this was hardly a novelty coming from him.

Riding out of Widecombe, we came to the Rugglestone Inn, a marvellous anachronism with no pub sign, no spirit licence and, since it was situated some way off a minor road and adorned with wooden shutters, no actual evidence to outsiders of its existence. It was the kind of pub where eighty-year-old shepherds drink bottled beer and talk about a neighbour who died in 1924. Entering the large, unlit courtyard, we sat, still mounted, enjoying the drinks Bob had inevitably conjured up. It was at this juncture that the first diversion occurred. One of the horses started to fidget and his rider, attempting to settle him one-handed, took him for a gentle walk up the courtyard. He had ridden only a few yards when he said something approximating to 'GURP'; the consequence of having tangled throat-first with a wire washing line which spanned the courtyard at rider height. This, naturally, was a source of great amusement for those of us with unruptured Adam's apples, but more was to come.

An elderly local gentleman, full of the joys of alcohol, emerged from the inn to weave his way across the courtyard to the outside loo. As he dished and plaited his way among the horses, it apparently dawned on his scrumpied sub-concious that progress would be easier with something to hold on to, so he solemnly took hold of the nearest bridle and proceeded on his way with a surprisingly cooperative horse in tow. Whether the horse's lady rider would normally have been so cooperative is open to question, but she had a nearly full glass in one hand, and was partially anaesthetised both by her own previous intake and sheer surprise. As the rest of us watched in gallant and silent fascination, the elderly gent and his entourage made their stately way towards the loo, and disappeared en mass through its cavernous doorway; the lady rider ducking neatly at the appropriate moment.

The Beginner's Horse

He's very warm and hairy and he wobbles quite a lot
He sort of swaggers when he walks, and bumps about in trot.
He stops and starts at random and the steering seems awry
And he stares round at my wellie with a surly, jaundiced eye.
I really hope he's friendly and he doesn't rear or buck
And then, maybe, I'll stay on top, with superglue and luck.

The Riding Lesson

Gyrating round and round the ring
In orbit most elliptical
I think that I've tried everything
I cannot stop this horse at all.

Helpless, collapsed with vertigo
The poor instructor lies distraught
While suddenly, the great truth dawns —
I should have been an astronaut.

FREE WALK ON A LONG REIN.

RIDING CLUB QUIZZES

BEING A LITTLE OUT OF THE RIDING CLUB mainstream these days, I am not sure whether inter-club quizzes are as prevalent as they once were. In the seventies, in the London area, they were a winter institution. Although some were organised locally, on an informal basis, there was also a London-wide one, administered by the London Riding Club's Liaison Committee. This quiz was seen, in part, as having an educational function, and was taken just as seriously as the mounted competitions — at least by the snotty North London Clubs.

My own clubs, the South London Saddle Club (drinking first, equitation second) and the GLC Staff Riding Club (drinking first, equitation nowhere) had rather different attitudes towards The Quiz; indeed, it was somewhat surprising that either entered teams, although both did, on a regular basis. The motivation for so doing was probably the strong sense of the absurd which, for example, led to John Cherrington actually being Chairman of the Liaison Committee for a while — a situation strongly akin to having a piranha fish dwelling in a lavatory bowl. Anyway, the committees of both clubs made annual decisions to enter teams, initial selection being based upon the twin criteria of which club members appeared gullible enough to be conned into participation, and which had exhibited know-all tendencies and needed letting down a peg or two. However, it was usually necessary to modify the teams somewhat because, given the average character of club members, no-one would actually agree to take part unless they were given guarantees that a couple of their best drinking mates — or someone they fancied — would also be in the team.

The one irony was that both clubs had a few very knowledgeable people on their books — often dissolute eccentrics who had achieved equestrian fame but had forgotten to cancel their membership, or people who had been made honorary members or Vice Presidents during acts of Machiavellian wheedling. These luminaries could sometimes be persuaded to appear as team members although they, too, usually insisted upon the presence of team mates they could happily drink with or lust after.

On average, therefore, a team from either club would consist of an equestrian (flawed) genius, a drunk, a sex object and a new member who had been too naive to say 'no'. The quiz itself usually took place in the social centre of the organising club's workplace; normally an imposing but hard to find office block in town. 'Our' team would foregather at a mutually convenient pub before travelling mob-handed to the quiz venue, where they would head straight for the subsidised bar. Seated at corner tables would be knots of earnest North London club members, sipping soft drinks and testing each other on the finer points of stable management. Intermittently, soft, liturgical chants would emanate from them — 'a foul condition of the cleft of the frog' — as they learnt the BHS Manual by rote. Spurning such use of last minute revision time, our team would be telling dirty jokes, making plans for the Christmas social, and arguing about whose round it was.

The quiz itself would have a surreal quality. This would not be due entirely to the antics of our team — indeed, the underlying reason would be the bizarre nature of some of the questions. I was once asked, right at the start of a quiz, when the saddle was first used. I plucked an answer completely out of the air, and now have no recollection of the date I gave, or the basis for my giving it. Much to my astonishment, my answer was deemed correct, which was something of a miracle because I still don't understand how

anyone can be *that* sure. (I bet some entrepreneurial Asiatic nomad took out a patent *aeons* before any saddle that even Elwyn Hartley Edwards has heard about: 'Genghis's Patent Goolie Saver. Rape and pillage in comfort and luxury on hand-tooled yak skin. Only three goats and a wife from selected outlets'.)

On another occasion, right at the end of a quiz, I was asked 'What is slot?' When I replied, correctly, that it was the track of a deer, the quizmistress nearly fell off her stool in amazement, and so did everyone else. Apparently, I was the only one present who had ever heard the term. Quite what it has to do with equitation I do not know, but the general knowledge round of these quizzes often made reference to archaic hunting terms. This, in itself, gave rise to some peculiar moments. I recall the question 'What is a thruster?' and the official answer 'One who rides hard to hounds', but had best draw a veil over the reply to 'What is giving tongue?'.

Given the lack of balance between such questions and 'Name the sequence of legs in left canter', it is not suprising that scoring would proceed fitfully. The well-bred members of the North London teams tended to know seven or eight of the nine rules of feeding, and were able to name most parts of a double bridle, but they were hazy on key issues such as the venue for the Cheltenham Gold Cup or the name of that year's Derby winner. Our naive member would get some points for most answers, on the grounds that they would be so vague and convoluted that the quizmaster could not be sure whether the question had been answered or not. Our sex object would do very well or badly, depending on whether the chemistry between them and the quizmaster/mistress was based upon lust or jealousy. Our drunk would cloud the issue with alcohol-inspired logic:

'How would you pick out a horse's feet?'

'Ah, they'd be the flat bits at the bottoms of his legs' and

'What is the point of hock?'

'Well, it goes quite nicely with a chicken salad' being two examples which spring to mind.

More confusing, however, would be the exchanges between the equestrian genius and the quizmaster, with the former putting the latter right on the finer points of equine metabolism and biomechanics. Indeed, answers initially disputed by the quizmaster would invoke fifteen-minute lectures: 'I know Hayes says. . . but latest research in America suggests that. . . . Actually, a friend of mine is on the working party and. . .'

Depending upon the resolution or otherwise of the quizmaster, this sort of thing sometimes took us dangerously close to winning through to the final; a traumatic prospect which would have done enormous damage to our credibility. Fortunately, such shame was repeatedly avoided at the last minute by our equestrian genius getting the last question — usually 'Who is the chairman of the British Horse Society?' — hopelessly wrong. At this juncture, the team would heave a corporate sigh of relief — and go off to the pub.

Prix Caprilli

Prix Caprilli
Is very silly
Riders seated erect
To no great effect
There — one has departed
Quite hopelessly carted
But — needless to mention —
Still sat at attention
And, with that fixed grin
Will quite probably win
But I don't mind confiding
I'd rather watch riding.

COWBOY OF THE YEAR AWARD

SOME YEARS AGO, NICKY AND I WISELY introduced the Cowboy of the Year Award to the GLC Riding Club. I say wisely wisely, because it was the one trophy for which there was always fierce competition. The trophy was a replica Colt revolver, and it was awarded annually for the greatest act of ineptitude in the presence of an equine. In pursuit of this coveted award, club members backed a pony and trap into a brand new Jag., fell repeatedly from a stationary horse and — in the infamous person of Joyce Bellamy — chased an escaped donkey round the streets of Croydon at 2 a.m. clad only in a nightdress and with *police assistance*. I never won the Cowboy Of The Year Award, and the reason for this is that sheer irresolution prevented my seizing my golden opportunity.

This is the story of my craven failure. The GLC Staff Sports Club held a major sports day at Crystal Palace stadium, and our club had the bright idea of setting up a promotional stand. To assist the promotion Joyce — yes, her again — brought along her prize-winning Dales mare, Elsie. Now, before travelling down to the sports day, I had gone for a lunchtime drink with a workmate, whose idea of a 'quick one' was as many pints of Young's Special as he could artlessly extract from any vague acquaintances. By the time I reached Crystal Palace I was having an out-of-body experience — and then I found that the least reputable members of the club had discovered a subsidised bar.

When Joyce offered me a ride at about four o'clock,

I had drunk sufficient to be in that condition which conveys an external appearance of sobriety. I mounted and wandered around awhile, rejoining the others just as a great coup was announced: someone had persuaded the Leader Of The Council (gasp) and his wife to come and visit our stand! The Leader's wife was — unbelievably — wearing a massive hat decorated with artificial fruit. And she came up to make a fuss of Elsie. Who eyed up the fruit. All my basest instincts cried out 'Let the reins slip through your fingers. Ultimate notoriety can be yours.'

But, dithering in an alcoholic haze, I didn't.

Throughout my whole riding career, I have never been so ashamed of myself — except when Dave Mortlock beat me in the egg and spoon race at our Christmas gymkhana. But *he* was so drunk he could have carried nitro-glycerine safely in rising trot.

Cowboy Equitation

In cowboy equitation the horse must be well bent
In different directions and to varying extent
His head must point to heaven and his tail must point to 'C'
He must plait and dish on different legs and forge diagonally.

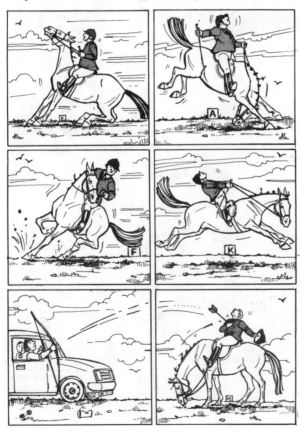

Lines on a Riding Club Dressage Competition

Oh, the Masters gyrate with great presence and grace
And immaculate collection and flexion
And they set a great store (both for Art and for score)
On maintaining correct bend and direction.
Their extensions are grand and their changes of hand
Bring a murmer of awe from the crowd;
Their seats supple and strong and their legs still and long
And their horses are agile and proud.
They can rein-back, passage, pirouette or go large
Flying changes don't cause any trouble
They could do it bareback on a racehorse or hack
In a headcollar, snaffle or double.

Choosing a Horse

Equine selection
Requires circumspection
Don't ever buy one with odd feet
He needs to have four
No less and no more
Or else he won't look very neat.

Pasterns and hocks
Knee joints, fetlocks and docks
All help make the horse function nicely
But the last tends to smell
And the rest sometimes swell
So it's best not to check them precisely.

'WITH THIS RANGE OF ACCESSORIES, OF COURSE HE'S AN
ALL-ROUNDER.'

STABLE MANAGEMENT

ALL THAT STUFF ABOUT FEEDING AND MUCKING OUT comes as second nature to us leathery, weather-beaten jump-' em-out-of-your-stride characters. The problem is, it can sometimes get a little confused...

Shortly after acquiring the shaggy and boisterous Ebony, I went to ride her one winter's evening. Before grooming her, I skipped out a couple of piles of droppings, dolloping them into one of the black plastic buckets provided for the purpose. These buckets were of the same type as those used for mixing feed, so the staff had helpfully painted the word SHIT on them to avoid confusion. I left the half-full bucket to the right of the stable door, thinking it would be convenient later, if Ebony produced more dung while I was untacking, rugging-up and generally tucking her in for the night.

While I was in the floodlit school, the stable proprietor departed for the evening, switching off the exterior stable block lights, but leaving the internal light of Ebony's box on, to guide us back after our evening of haute école. On returning to the box, I did all the requisite fiddling about and, noting that Ebony had not produced any more droppings, I picked up the bucket outside and slung it onto the darkened dung heap. My only remaining task was to feed her, and I was somewhat surprised to find that her dinner had not been made up as usual. However, I knew that the yard proprietor had been in a hurry and, reflecting that anyone can forget occasionally, I mixed a feed myself.

The next morning, phoning the yard on another matter, I felt inclined to remonstate gently: 'By the way, you forgot to make Ebony's dinner up last night'. 'No I didn't − I found it on top of the muck heap this morning'. Having tidily emptied the dung bucket, she had left the feed in exactly the same place.

At least, on that occasion, I had the excuses of darkness and coincidence. Down at my friend Terry's yard, I was charged with taking the erratic Bumble for some 'schooling'. 'If you don't get him too hot, he can have his feed when he comes back' said Lynda, the head girl.

Somewhat to my surprise, Bumble took quite well to going round in ever-decreasing circles, and I was rather pleased with myself upon our return. I was also rather pushed for time and preoccupied so, having checked him over (for brain damage and so on), I picked up the bucket outside his box and lobbed it into his manger without a second glance.

'How was he?', called Lynda as I hurried past.

'Oh, quite good actually — by the way, I've put his feed in'.

'What feed? I haven't done them yet'.

'Well, it was outside his box — I assumed it must be his'. We hurried across the yard, both puzzled. I reached the box first, and looked in.

'That's funny, he doesn't seem very keen on it'. When we investigated, we discovered why. Even greedy, quirky horses do not think much of a bucketful of soiled shavings and droppings.

JOYCE AND HER DALES

My friend Joyce is a native pony nutter whose life's work is to extol the virtues of the native breeds. There is a couplet — often reproduced after homilies on horse management — which goes along the lines of

Be to his virtues ever kind
Be to his faults a little blind.

Well, if it's wilful and hairy, Joyce is prepared to go much further, in both directions.

While she owns a bevy of assorted ponies — many rescued from unpleasant situations and restored to mental and physical health — Joyce's favourite native is the Dales. Dales ponies (ponies — hah!) are huge, hirsute and 'fun-loving' (if you think of them as ponderous pack animals you should try sitting on one while the hailstones drum on the roof of the covered school) and therefore, in Joyce's eyes, they represent equine perfection. In her hands, too, they tend to thrive. Her old mare, Elsie, had a long and distinguished career in the show ring and, when she retired, Joyce bought a youngster, Jamie. He, predictably, became the apple of her eye and, when she was in the throws of backing him she, typically, conned me into 'assisting'. This was the result:

For the purpose of schooling a Dales
You need courage and tumblers of scotch
And a whip and a chair and some armour
And a bevy of sadists to watch.

For the purpose of schooling a Dales
You need patience and humour and tact
And a stout pair of boots and a cudgel
And a 'chute when the creature is backed.

For the purpose of schooling a Dales
You need hands like a navvy at least
And a seat like a heavyweight wrestler
In order to stay on the beast.

For the purpose of schooling a Dales
You need all sorts of quirks by the ton
But what you need most is endurance
And a very bizarre sense of fun.

PAS DE DALES.

'SUCH LOVELY, POWERFUL QUARTERS.'

Joyce's weakness for Dales has the effect of her ascribing Dalesness to any bulky, shaggy equine who exhibits nous, aptitude and a robust attitude towards life. Should the equine be of uncertain parentage, she concludes (rightly) that this strengthens her case. A few years ago, I became part owner of a cob mare, Ebony. She had three interests in life; eating, jumping and galloping, all of which she performed with equal enthusiasm. In the summer, she had a fine, glossy coat like a sea lion, and in the winter she grew a coat that would have made a yak look bald. She also had a very high, active trot. We did not know her breeding, but it was almost certain that she was a native/Thoroughbred cross and she *could have* been part Dales. Joyce, naturally, would have none of the could have; the mare won rosettes, she was hairy, she was ravenous. Joyce delighted in all reports of Ebonyesque mischief, and claimed her as one of the chosen few. Although I had no real objection to this, I felt honour-bound to put up some show of resistance, even though the following is a pack of lies:

37

Stop saying my mare is a Dales
She's shiny and slim and well bred
And she doesn't really have feather
And a thick winter coat and big head.

Stop saying my mare is a Dales
She's seven-eighths T.B. at least
She's a riding club horse of the best sort
Not some shaggy M. and M. beast.

Stop saying my mare is a Dales
She is ladylike, dainty and sweet
She is swan-necked and doe-eyed and sylphlike
And balletic and light on her feet.

Stop saying my mare is a Dales
A label which only applies
To mammoths and Jamies and suchlike
Of truly preposterous size.

Coping

The late Barbara Woodhouse undoubtedly had a way with animals, albeit sometimes rather eccentric. A few years ago, a television series showed her dealing with behavioural problems in horses, with varying degrees of success, but consistent ingenuity. Her solutions included lassoing a horse and blowing up his nose (apparently a South American Indian ploy), and devising a pulley system for loading, of which Archimedes would have been proud. The series inspired the following:

If your 'orse is a bugger and won't come when you ask
Thee mustn't get upset with 'im, nor take the beast to task
You mustn't throw no bricks at 'im or 'it 'im with a rake
And to chase 'im with a hunting whip would be a grave mistake
The answer to 'is foibles isn't curses, yells or blows —
Just lasso 'im with a bit of string and whisper up 'is nose.

If your 'orse is a bugger and won't box off to the meet
But stands and stares, lays back 'is ears and plants 'is ruddy feet
Don't shove no broomstick up 'is arse, don't push and strain and heave
Till your arms 'ave turned to jelly, you've gone puce and cannot breathe
Just get yourself a lunge line, and some sugar if you wish
And, if you still can't load 'im, you can play 'im like a fish.

THE YOUNG BARBARA WOODHOUSE PERFECTING HER
TECHNIQUE OF BLOWING UP THE HORSE'S NOSE.

Gadgets

My mare goes in a martingale; I really don't know why
But all my friends have fitted them, and, therefore, so have I.
And next I'll try some draw reins, they'll make her flex much faster
Until, with head stuck up her arse, she'll look just like her master.

CONDEMNED TO WANDER FOR EVER IN LIMBO, THE INVENTOR
OF THE PATENT BENDING TACKLE GETS HIS ETERNAL
COMEUPPANCE.

COMMUNICATION

THE FLAWED AND FRAGILE COMMUNICATION which usually exists between horse and rider is at least less tenuous than the even more flawed and fragile communication which often takes place between riders, or between one rider's brain and mouth. From politicians, one expects contradictory nonsense; from overexcited, cerebrally challenged sports commentators one expects inarticulate blundering, but in the horse world there is a kind of dislocated logic which I term equiwarp. My theory is that this could be triggered by the pressure of close-fitting hard hats reducing blood circulation to the brain; on the other hand, it could be a manifestation of a congenital condition which creates a predisposition towards taking up riding. Is equiwarp a cause or effect of equitation? This is a question upon which those undertaking equine studies with psychology at Agricultural College can doubtless write complex dissertations. To help them on their way, here are a few case studies:

My first experience of equiwarp — indeed, that which made me aware of the phenomenon — occurred when a riding club member said, after a rather fraught Prix Caprilli test, that she had 'given the right aids, but the horse didn't halt'. Quite so. I'm sure that all of us have been there in our own minds at some time or another. It strikes me as being a wonderful line with which to attempt to placate a puce-faced Field Master who is rapidly vanishing into the background.

Another early example was given by my friend Marian, a sober (usually), sensible, safety conscious instructor, with

44

LOOK, EQUIWARP CAN BE PHYSICAL
AS WELL AS MENTAL.

many years exerience of teaching novice riders. Gamely, she
told the story against herself. Teaching a new class, she told
them to take their feet out of the stirrups and cross them
over. There was a dull thud and one pupil, still cross-legged,
lay on the ground wearing a puzzled frown. Surely, this was
one of those cases where there is justification for asking
'Is it them or me?'

There is one form of equiwarp which may spring from
either wishful thinking or overconditioning by horse dealers.
We all know that a dealer's first question 'How much do you
want to spend?' lays the foundation for elasticity of the price
of anything vaguely suitable, and that all horses ages are
strictly approximate, but it is also true that, to some extent,
horses can shrink or grow according to requirement. Thus,
when Vicky advertised a 17 hand heavyweight hunter in
Horse and Hound as a 17 hand heavyweight hunter, she had a
stream of prospective purchasers arrive from far and wide,

who took one look at the animal and said, sniffily and bristling with the resentment of those-whose-time-has-been-wasted 'Oh no, he's *far* too big'. Since Vicky was, herself, a little into dealing, there is some sense of accidental natural justice here.

However, a similar thing happened to Denise, who is not a dealer. She advertised a horse for loan; he, too, was 17 hands — a Thoroughbred — and advertised as such. A girl and her instructor turned up, saw him in his box, saw him ridden and then the girl rode him herself. A loan agreement was made, and the horse went off to his new home. A couple of weeks later, the girl phoned to say she wanted to send him back. The sole reason she gave was that he was 'too big'. Subsequent examination established that he was still 17 hands.

It was also Denise who told me that she had been walking a hunter trial course with a mutual friend who tends to have a very precise approach to life. (It is rumoured that he takes a theodolite when he goes course walking). He said, of a chair fence, that he was not sure how to approach it, and wondered whether he should 'try to jump the front part or the back part'. Now Denise would not pretend to have great technical expertise in such matters, but she does have a certain pragmatism. 'If I were you', she said, 'I'd try to jump the whole thing'.

However, my very favourite example of equiwarp is not drawn from personal experience and, since it concerns an Irish jockey, I can only hope earnestly that it is not apocryphal. While legging the jockey up to ride in a 2 mile 6 furlong hurdle race, the trainer opined that the horse would be a certainty if the race were over 3 miles. 'Sure', said the jockey, 'I'll take him round the outside then'.

Reason for Sale —
Owner no Time

This poem was inspired by a lot of horse owners I know —
not all of them women:

So, I've finally mucked out and plaited
And given my horse a shampoo
Cleaned my tack, drunk some tea, had a fag and — let's see
Spent at least half an hour in the loo.
And I've had a good gossip with Mandy
Well, Pam and that blacksmith of hers!
Mandy said for a fact they'd been caught in the act
And with Pam wearing nothing but spurs.

Now I've just got to empty my barrow
And give the New Zealand a clean
And point out to Tony that his daughter's pony
Is looking a little bit lean
And I should try to sort out that poll guard
I think it should really go back
Though it fits him a treat and looks perfectly neat
I have never quite liked him in black.

And now to get into my jodhpurs
And take my horse out for a ride
I am sure, were he fit, we could win quite a bit
But I just don't have time on my side.
Gosh, it's quarter to seven already
And I've said I'll go out with a friend
I've no time for a hack, I would never get back —
But I **must** try to ride this weekend.

'IT'S NOT THAT I DON'T HAVE TIME TO GROOM HIS MANE...
HE'S RASTAFARIAN.'

VICES OBSERVED IN RIDERS

Brigadier Kurt Albrecht, former Commander of the Spanish Riding School, wrote: 'Most of the cases of resistance or even open rebellion by the horse to the rider's commands are founded upon that most human of all human attributes, which is to forgive one's own weaknesses and to be intolerant of the weaknesses of others'. While there is much food for thought in this remark for all us riders, it also led me to ponder:

WINDSUCKING.   Observed in male riders whose private parts come into sudden, violent contact with the pommel of their saddle. Characterised by a sharp intake of breath, accompanied by grey pallor and watering eyes. Dismounted, the windsucker will tend to plait in walk, and show marked lack of impulsion. The condition can sometimes be alleviated by massage, although such treatment may invite habit-forming repetition. Confirmed windsuckers are best fitted with cricket boxes and reschooled to improve posture, especially when jumping.

Windsucking.   Plaiting.

WEAVING. Often seen in riders who have recently been treated for crib-biting. Sometimes also observed in mounted form by apparently dyslexic riders who interpret the dressage command 'Enter at A, proceed to X' as meaning 'Ride a serpentine of uncertain dimensions and location'.

Weaving.

Cure for weaving.

CRIB-BITING. Rider hangs onto dashboard of car with teeth on way to competition. May also break into cold sweat, whimper and mutter about 'that bloody great drop fence'. Droppings often loose and watery, and sometimes involuntary. A cure can sometimes be effected by administering copious quantities of neat spirits.

Crib-biting.   Anti-cribbing device.

BALKING, BUCKING AND JIBBING. Various reactions to being told of a sudden increase in livery charges.

Balking.

The cure — counter-change of hand to husband (where applicable).

SHYING. In maiden lady riders, characterised by blushing and murmering 'Oh, I say', when oversexed male instructor spends excessive amount of time adjusting upper thigh position.

In male riders, characterised by sudden silence when subjected to explicit overtures from bevy of voracious girl grooms.

Shying.

Shoulder-in; a cure for shying.

BOLTING. In male riders, a secondary reaction to shying.
In impecunious livery owners, a secondary reaction to balking, bucking and jibbing.
In competitive riders, the swallowing sideways of an entire jumbo hot dog on hearing their number called unexpectedly early.

Bolting.

Bolting is prevented by wearing a muzzle.

REARING.   Normally observed in male riders to hounds, this is characterised by following a lady rider with an especially shapely bottom in mesmerised fashion across the roughest and most difficult country. Although, from a social viewpoint, it is usually considered a vice, from an equestrian viewpoint it often has the virtue of making the rider appear more proficent than he really is because, being so absorbed by the object of his desire, he leaves his horse to his own devices, rather than pulling him about in ham-fisted fashion.

Rearing.

Action to cure a confirmed rearer.

The Cherrington Method

My friend John Cherrington is (I hate to admit) actually quite a sensitive and considerate rider for a 6 ft 4 in ex-rugby player. When, judging him in a club dressage test, I wrote 'mindless brutality is no substitute for equitation' in the rider comments, I was only half serious. I was, therefore, deeply offended when he asked 'How would you know?', so I decided to pursue the matter further:

When man first tamed horses in B.C. Umpteen
The first Riding Master appeared on the scene
And down through the ages, as riding advanced
His theories were studied, revised and enhanced.

He claimed the first thing you must do to improve
Is to climb safely on and then make your horse move
Now this caused great debate — some said 'squeeze', some said 'kick'
Some said 'swear at the bugger and then use your stick'

And some used rowelled spurs or electrified whips
And some used their heels; others wiggled their hips
But the Cherrington method, devised in the scrum
Is to shove it along with your head up its bum.

Now, once having started, you'll wish to progress
While you stay on the back of the beast, more or less
And the Cherrington method of staying astride
Requires very strong teeth and suspension of pride.

58

And eventually, maybe, you'll feel that you ought
To make some sort of effort to make the horse halt
And, despite abject failure with curbs, gag and grakle
You'll stop a Shire dead with a Cherrington tackle.

For Jo

A lady should be most discreet
When making full use of her seat
Overt pelvic thrusting
Sets gentlemen lusting
So aids must be subtle and neat.

Showing Enthusiasm

Livery yards are strange places; the horse owners equivalent of masonic lodges. They are places where people come dressed in the uniform of their sect (The Antediluvian Order Of Waxed Jackets, Chaps and Kickers) and spend time in ceremonies which appear impenetrable to the uninitiated, but which have deep significance for the devotees.

A prime example is the ceremony of Looking Through Schedules, which takes an impressive two-cups-of-coffee worth of time, and must be accompanied by a deeply furrowed brow. 'Gosh', thinks the uninitiated observer 'that rider is going to a show every week for the next four months'. Not so: the Incantation Of Dismissal begins, an impressive vehicle for the human imagination, which produces a string of highly original reasons for *not* going to the shows. The reasons never include any as crass, craven or mundane as the fences being too big or the competition too fierce, but they may include the arena surface being the wrong colour, or the possibility that someone from whom the speaker decided not to buy a horse five years previously might conceivably be judging. (By way of personal digression, it is my boast that I stand aloof from all this. My own decision-making about shows is based upon the presence or absence of the following: a beer tent; a caterer selling both sausages containing real meat and good home-made cakes; decent, non-collapsible loos — see Hunter Trialling — which have been emptied within the last decade.

Occasionally, through sheer lack of mental agility, a horse owner will fail the Incantation Of Dismissal and actually decide to go to a show. This leads to the ritual of Getting A Boxload, an unpleasant and protracted business in which unreasonable pressure is brought to bear on other, reluctant, owners. A standard chant used for this is a high-pitched, wheedling and repetitious 'Oh, go on, you said you'd come to the next one and I can't afford a box by myself and I did lend you that tail guard last week'. Given that anyone who fails the Incantation of Dismissal is treated as a pariah, there is great resistance to this chant but, eventually, one or two of the less hardened or spirited owners may crack, at which point Getting A Boxload is superceded by the farcical ritual of Trying To Find A Box.

Trying To Find A Box consists of two Acts. In Act I, other horse owners with their own boxes are approached, and are required to make the standard response 'Of course you could borrow it, but it has no tax/wheels/brakes, otherwise I'd be using it myself'. (The first part of this response is invariably true, but the latter is an artless lie; the box is there primarily to be tinkered with on summer days, as a means of evading having to school the horse). Act II consists of phoning round local horse transport firms to confirm that they are already booked. Really advanced practitioners of Trying To Find A Box may also phone a distant firm, so that they can report with a due blend of diffidence and sadness 'Well, I've found a box, but I'm afraid it's got to come from Taunton'.

When Trying To Find A Box ends in failure, it is time for The Mourning, a present day equivalent of the role of the chorus in Greek Tragedies. For The Mourning, participants gather round the table in the common room, staring sullenly into half-empty cups. At intervals, Enquirers enter and ask 'Is anyone going to ...?, to which The Mourners respond in unison 'Love to have gone, couldn't get a box'. (Some older Mourners, with classical educations, tend to suffix this response with 'Woe, woe, woe', but this is generally considered archaic nowadays.) Individual Mourners then take turns to outline the fact that their horse would have 'definitely gone clear/won the Working Hunter/been placed in the Novice 12.'

On rare occasions, the person Trying To Find A Box may learn, worryingly, that one is available. The reason for worry is that, to be available, a box usually has to be either exorbitantly expensive, devoid of several key parts or driven by a dypsomaniac with no sense of time or direction. The more surprising its availability, the more likely it is that all three conditions pertain. However, while it is considered legitimate to enquire about cost, it is not so easy for the person Trying To Find A Box to address the other issues. Asking 'Do the brakes work?' can, with the surlier type of driver, invite a future demonstration which results in four horses doing ninety degree lateral work through the living compartment, while questions such as 'Do you put whisky on your cornflakes?' and 'Do you know when Sunday is?' are socially difficult. Therefore, once it has been established that hiring the box will not entail group bankruptcy, there is nothing for the enquirer to do but say 'Oh, great, can we book you then?' while trying to disguise the dull shock of unexpected commitment. The waves of this dull shock will, in due course, oscillate outwards to afflict those unfortunates who constitute The Boxload, and their gleeful cries of 'Oh, great, well done', can be interpreted, by the initiated, as meaning 'Oh, Heavens, I hope it gets rained off' or even, in extreme cases, 'I hope that damn horse of mine puts his back out again before Sunday'.

Usually, these anxieties are set to rest in ironic fashion; the convoluted processes which lead to Finding A Box will have taken so long that, by the time entry fees and forms (duly soaked with blood and sweat) have been posted, the relevant classes will be closed. The relief when they are returned marked 'Sorry, class full' will be tangible, but the event will inevitably provoke a second outbreak of Mourning: 'Just when the ground has dried out'; 'Just when I'd got is back sorted out'; 'The judge there always likes him'...

Evidence, indeed, that joy cometh in The Mourning.

For Jacqui

I got a one at dressage
It made me feel just great
Cos only bores get threes and fours
And jammy sods get eight.

I wasn't 'insufficient'
I wasn't 'fairly bad'
For such are minor failings which
Are generally, just sad.

And getting nought at dressage
Is simply copping out
Craven capitulation which
One cannot brag about.

But I got one at dressage
And earned it through and through
It's there in black and white to prove
I'm classier than you.

DRESSAGE – THE TRUTH

REPRODUCED BELOW IS PART OF THE PREFACE to *Riding a Dressage Test*, a book I co-wrote with Terry Colgate (he knows about dressage: I can do joined up writing). In pretentious moments, I have read a number of books on classical equitation (to little obvious effect), and it remains my proud boast that *Riding a Dressage Test* is the only text which addresses the truth as defined in the introduction to the book you are reading now.

Those readers who have participated in inter-club dressage competitions on hired horses will know beyond doubt that I am right in this:

Many riders, especially those who are not horse owners or convinced dressage enthusiasts, do not enter their first test because of a conviction that they have elevated equitation to an art form; they do so because someone badgers them into 'having a go', or because it is an unavoidable precursor to the 'exciting' phases of a horse trial.

Having succumbed to coercion, or bowed to the inevitable, the rider is confronted with a test sheet which seems to consist by turns of impossibly complicated and hopelessly inadequate instructions. Attempts to commit the test to memory result in midnight incantations, ritual dances in the garden and increasingly worried neighbours.

Eventually, the day dawns when the competitor must try to translate the cause of insomnia into a display of equine grace – possibly on an unfamiliar horse who looks, and moves, as though there is a prepotent element of dinosaur in his pedigree.

Two minutes before the start of the test, total amnesia replaces the black despair of the practise arena, and the rider drifts through the movements like a sleepwalker in a maze, to be damned with faint praise by a judge who is desperate for a cup of coffee.

The preface goes on to say that the book is about '...how to go about riding a test whilst minimising the traumas outlined...' I know it is bragging, but I like to think that wisdom, as well as fear of the Trade Descriptions Act, caused the use of the word 'minimising' rather than 'eradicating'. After all, how many of you affiliated-dressage-people-riding-warmbloods-at-medium-level can claim, in all honesty, never to have experienced one of those pre-test panic attacks which begin 'Oh my God, where's A?'

The Dressage Test

All we, like sheep, have gone astray
(Amnesia sets in at 'A')
And, turning down the centre line
I rode a perfect serpentine.

Perverse and foolish oft I strayed —
The halt at 'X' was much delayed
And, if he had not deigned to budge
I would have halted on the judge.

I wandered through the wilderness
Twixt 'M' and 'K' in great distress
At random, on the verge of tears
For what seemed long, infernal years.

Till exiting, by chance, at least
Confused, exhausted and downcast
By accident it came to pass
That I had won the freestyle class.

Elevation

'STOP IN THE NAME OF THE BHS DRESSAGE GROUP — YOUR
BRASSIERE DOES NOT COMPLY WITH THE RULES FOR
RIDERS' DRESS.'

The following lines were inspired by the recent profusion of
adverts in the equestrian press for 'minimal bounce' bras:

It can be quite a bore watching dressage —
A succession of leathery crones
Going through stilted paces with miserable faces
And rattle of brittling bones.

But then into the ring bounces Bella
And Bella's not wearing a bra
Her trot work shows great elevation
And Bella looks bound to go far.

She piaffes and passages with passion
And her team mates are bursting with pride
But so are her show shirt and jacket
Quite undone by the fervour inside.

See her ride pirouettes with great gusto
While her chest swings in several directions
There are cheers long and loud from the chaps in the crowd
And the judges are sporting erections.

As she finally leaves the arena
She's awarded a standing ovation
With the judges — poor men — shouting 'encore' and 'ten'
Bar the one who's expired of elation.

Course Walking

Well, at least I've found out where the start is
But where does the course go from here?
It's hard enough kicking and pushing
Without also having to steer.
Number one — no surprise — is a rustic
And the mare's bound to have a good look
I shall give her a slap if the cow tries to nap
And we'll clear it by hook or by crook.
Now you need to turn right to the second
Though you have to start off in left lead
But let's not get excited — she's never united
Just skid, take a pull and proceed,
And the third is a straightforward oxer
But the colour scheme's really quite vile
So my aesthetic mission is quick demolition
Then onward, post haste, to the stile.
Now the trouble with stiles is, they're narrow
While my mare is exceedingly wide
I can see that we might be suspended mid-flight
With a wing firmly stuck to each side.
But if we stay wedged there'll be time faults
Which are something I really don't need
So we'll strive to explode out of Pegasus mode
And bear down on the dyke at great speed.
There, I should try to get off the forehand
But I'd say that's a long shot at best
There'll be rattle and clatter — the odd pole may shatter

Then onward, to tackle the rest.
There's a run up the hill to the double
And I hope that I see a good stride
It's been built rather long and if one comes in wrong
The spread out is bowel-movingly wide.
Change the rein, once again to the triple
Where appraisal brings moments of dread
If she stands off and dives we will both need nine lives
So I'd better keep hold of her head.
And next — oh what fun — comes the water
All aglow from the rays of the sun
Our spectacular version of total immersion
Will give the spectators some fun.
And expect whoops of glee from the scorer
As a latter day Flood is observed
One takes pride in a round where a jump judge is drowned
And in faults which are truly deserved.
Then the last, all lined up for the exit
And approached down the hill, is the wall
So it's 'seek and destroy' at the gallop — what joy —
It was worth coming here after all.

Hunter Trialling

It was a wet spring morning in Kent. It was a *very* wet spring morning, with the rain falling tirelessly out of a slate grey sky, just as it had done for days. It was a Sunday morning, when I had risen blearily before six, and been shocked into full consciousness by the realisation that I was definitely nuts, indeed, one might say, several nuts short of a hard feed. The schedule had said something about an all grass course with some good hedges. Good hedges there certainly were, but the all grass course would have made Passchendaele look like a billiard table. Furthermore, most of the hedges came after a ditch which looked like the Suez Canal's bigger, nastier brother. The horse I was to ride loved good hedges; he would hurtle towards them like a heat-seeking missile, and soar gloriously above them, landing far out over the other side, safely clear of tractor ruts, farm implements, jump stewards, courting couples and even concealed ditches. He did not, however, like ditches in plain view; neither was he suited by soft ground — and even an Irish Clerk of the Course would have described this as soft.

I was not, therefore, in a happy frame of mind. I was cold, wet, short of sleep, disillusioned, and becoming ever more fearful for my mental health. I also had a rotten belly ache.

Since the last was the only condition I could immediately alleviate, I went in search of the loo, and found a wooden edifice halfway up a slippery hillside. It was a loo which paralleled perfectly Shakespeare's description of Richard The

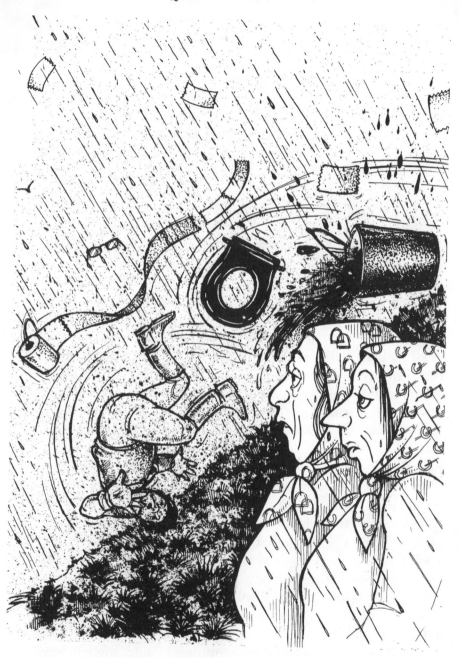

'THE PERILS OF AN INSECURE SEAT, CAMILLA.'

Third: 'Deformed, unfinished, sent before its time into this breathing world scarce half made up . . .' although I did not, at first, realise quite how perfect the parallel was. Firstly, there was no lock or catch on the lopsided door. Although this did not greatly concern me — some belly aches are beyond social nicety — I gave the door a good pull inward, in the hope that it would stick in place. In fact, I gave a couple of mighty heaves, which suceeded in getting the swollen, misshapen wood 'in the hole'. Secondly, there was no roof. I sat on a glorified bucket in the pouring rain and thought darkly that, while I might well be eliminated at that ditch, I was damned if I was going to disappear into its glutinous abyss without the horse.

After some minutes, having exorcised both my mental and physical demons, I attempted to leave. The door was stuck — *very* stuck. My mighty heaves had pulled it through its frame, and the combination of slipshod carpentry and swollen timber rendered it impossible to open. It was at this point that I became glad that there was no roof. Even in slippery riding boots, I would be able to climb out over the top, using the cross struts on the door like ladder rungs.

It was when I was astride the top of the door that I became aware of the drawbacks of having a loo positioned halfway up a hill, with the door on the downhill side. There was a sense of fatalism as I felt the whole thing topple over under my weight, and as I, the dying wooden structure and the glorified bucket rolled down the hillside in a bizarre, Wealden avalanche, I serenely accepted that it was just one of those days. Halfway down, we rolled past a horsy-faced woman in a headscarf, and her look of combined disgust and disbelief almost compensated for later elimination at the Suez Abyss.

Cross-country — the Truth (For Willie)

Walking through the dripping woodland
Squelching through the clinging mud
Thinking, though it may be slippery
One would rather splat than thud.
See the cavern of the coffin
See the dark, devouring ditch
See that drop — the dark lake lurking —
Feel oneself begin to twitch.

Numbed and trance-like, make the saddle
Then that surge of power beneath
Feel that eager, powerful movement
Feel a flood of great relief.
See his ears prick at the bullfinch
Feel him pumping in your hands
Feel that powerful thust of take-off
Not a tremor as he lands.

Afterwards, panache reviving:
'Thought the course rode really well
Organised him at the water
Otherwise just kicked like hell'.
From the cheering warmth of beer tent
Skill and courage shrink the course
Surely, such heroic rider
Didn't really need a horse.

EVENTING

THE WORD 'EVENTING' TENDS TO CONJURE UP images of the
coach park at Badminton, green-wellied loo queues, multi-
horse boxes with sponsors names emblazoned along their
sides, brilliantly talented riders of international repute
and immaculately gleaming household-name horses flying
through four part combinations of massive construction and
impossible dimensions. But it isn't all like that.

My first experience of the sharp end of eventing came
when I went to Crookham Horse Trials as part of Carol's
entourage of friends, helpers and dogs. Since she had four
horses and an entourage of about eleven (excluding the
dogs), she rented overnight stabling for the horses, and we
swept out the horse box and lived in that and a mini van,
the premise being that forty quid for stabling was a lot
cheaper than B and B for the entourage. Carol's sidekick,
Bert, mixed job lots of beans and mash in a spare feed
bucket, and we all huddled together out of the chill of the
driving spring rain, and told each other what an adventure
it all was. Unfortunately, I and a guy named Roy were
banished to the mini van at bedtime. In addition to being
freezing cold, this had a ridged metal floor and — even fully
clothed — it proved too chilly and uncomfortable to sleep in
until we had walked down to the village pub for an hour's
serious rum drinking.

The next morning, after breakfast — beans and mash
again — we went to watch Carol's dressage test on Ziggy.
Ziggy was a beautifully bred Thoroughbred mare who Carol

had (typically) bought for £75 as an equine hatrack after her previous owners had attempted to starve her into submission. Carol had worked wonders with Ziggy but, although she was now in excellent condition, she still had several short circuits where her brain should have been. Halfway through a passable test, she responded to a request for lengthened strides with a truly spectacular rear, and the rest of the test was more remarkable for Carol's intrepid riding than for classical elegance. After the test, in need of a fag and a sit down, Carol asked me to hack Ziggy back to the stables; an opportunity I rather strangely leapt at. Waiting quietly to cross the road, apparently relaxed on a light rein contact, Ziggy suddenly conjured a second spectacular rear from nowhere, giving me a splendid view over Hampshire before returning to earth and walking calmly towards her box.

Ziggy's showjumping was relatively uneventful. In deference to her excitability, Carol jumped most of the fences from trot, but this was no problem since the mare had a truly enormous leap and could flow over a really big fence from nowhere. However, since Ziggy had never jumped a cross-country course before, it was no surprise that Carol went off to the bar, to seek inspiration in eight gins before attempting that phase.

While she was thus pursuing equestrian enlightenment, most of us went off to watch Bert's daughter tackle the cross-country on a horse named Cloud. In contrast to Ziggy, Cloud was quite a laid-back old soul, but not so laid-back as his rider, who spent her time in the start box walking on a long rein whilst devouring a kingsize burger; a feat of nonchalance I have not seen equalled by all the Todds, Starks, Greens and Lengs rolled together. Her subsequent steady clear round, while commendable for its equitation, was chiefly a triumph for the human digestive system.

Cloud's round, steady though it was, did not compare to Ziggy's. Round about her seventh gin, Carol decided to extend her game plan from the showjumping to the cross-country, and she duly proceeded to trot the whole way round, dutifully moving aside so as not to impair the progress of several other competitors who were tackling the course at more conventional speed. The commentator, a Tweseldown military type, was astounded — indeed, almost hysterical; I don't think he could decide whether to be outraged on behalf of the status quo or amused by Carol and Ziggy's stately progress.

After a round free of jumping, but not time, penalties, Carol proceeded to celebrate her success (survival) in the company of Major Paddy Burke. Paddy, who knew Carol well, was a vastly experienced and highly respected horseman and, like many such, he had a robust attitude towards enjoying life. Quite late in the evening, when he and Carol had been enjoying life for some time, she decided that he should meet her other horse, Jack, a big dapple grey Irish hunter type, and one of the nicest horses I have ever sat on. However, despite his virtues, Jack was not a pretty horse; he had a big plain head with a roman nose and odd markings. Although Carol loved him dearly, she was forever taking the mickey out of his looks and most commonly addressed him as 'you ugly sod'. On this occasion, her own personal gin lake moved her to place special emphasis both on Jack's abilities and his lack of physical beauty. Initially, in deference to Paddy's prowess as a judge, she introduced Jack as 'a good type of Irish hunter, but a bit plain', a summary with which Paddy readily agreed.

However, as discussion continued in Jack's box, Carol's descriptions of him became both more maudlin and extreme, while Paddy continued to nod agreement. By the time I slunk away, embarrassed, Carol was draped tearfully round Jack's neck muttering 'You're the kindest, most honest horse I've met, but you're so appallingly bloody ugly' and Paddy was saying something along the lines of 'Sure, he's a darlin' horse, but not a creature you'd be wanting to meet on a dark night'.

This introduction to eventing taught me two important facts about the sport. Firstly, it has a way of heightening one's perceptions and indeed, expanding reality, in much the same way that mescalin was believed to do in the early years of this century and, secondly, it gets you drinking in the best company.

Further to the latter point, my first competitive experience of eventing led me to realise that it is a sport at which one can easily bump into top people. The top person in question was Chris Collins, then a regular member of the British international team. Having taken a novice horse to Frensham, he had the misfortune to find himself in the same section as me. Prior to the cross-country, we were both giving our horses pipe-openers on converging courses, and it was only due to a mutual last moment glance upward that we avoided collision. Since it is normally considered bad equestrian practice to look down, I have always assumed that Mr. Collins had been checking his stopwatch. Me, I was just making sure that my horse was still there.

'THEY'RE SPECIALLY BRED FOR DRAGHUNTING — GIVES THE
LADIES A SPORTING CHANCE.'

TEAM CHASING

To DATE, I HAVE RIDDEN IN ONLY ONE TEAM CHASE, for the simple reason that I can never find three other people willing to make up a team. I am convinced that this has nothing to do with the fact that people baulk at the prospect of riding across country in close proximity to me (as if they could go fast enough!) and everything to do with the fact that most of my riding pals have become old and boring.

The one team chase that I did take part in was a local-level event held on a farm owned by the parents of Sara, a member of our club. In those days, everyone was young and enthusiastic, and quite excited by the prospect of forming a 'scratch' team. It was my good fortune, at that time, to be riding an excellent cross-country performer; the others were less well horsed. John was to ride the club's very own Melody — a fast and scopy, but novicy, nervous and erratic, mare. Pamela, who would literally ride anything vaguely equine, was on Kingston, who had been *given away* by a dealer. Kingston was athletic and able, but took a truly ferocious hold, and once succeeded in pulling the accomplished, resolute and (one has to add) substantial Pamela clean over his head. Nicky, small, fierce and determined not to be left out, had acquired Wellington, an honest enough, but rather nondescript creature who was perhaps a little out of his league.

There was much course walking and team planning. That is to say, I spent my time proposing (successfully) that, since my horse was the most experienced, we should lead.

John divided his time between pontificating about the line of approach to each fence and admiring the be-jodhpured bottoms of lady course walkers and Nicky, in consequence, divided her time between arguing about the lines of approach and aiming bruising uppercuts at John's lower ribs. Pamela, in all probability, spent her time swatting imaginary bunny rabbits with a rolled up schedule, because that was the sort of thing she did.

Halfway round the course was an unflagged hedge; an optional obstacle which could be jumped to save time and avoid a hairpin bend through a muddy gateway. It was not really very big but, in those days, it looked so. Consequently, there was some debate about whether we should jump it, the chief concern being Wellington's scope. Interpreting this as a slur on her own abilities, Nicky insisted that we should. Gradually, amidst much vituperation, all was decided. I would go first, giving Melody a lead, and Kingston, in third place, would do the same for Wellington. It was a watertight scheme. We lunched on burgers and fizzy drinks, well satisfied.

Over the first few fences, all went well. This means that, from my position at the head of affairs, I was in glorious ignorance of any problems the others may have been having. I think Wellington may have been a little fazed by it all, but his desire to keep up with the others overcame any reservations he may have had about the obstacles. Then we came to a tree trunk set in deep shadow, and Melody refused, causing Pamela to take evasive action. Since Kingston was beginning to 'hot up', this took the form of a large and rapid circle in the vicinity of the fence while Wellington, confused by the antics of his 'lead', ground to a halt in a welter of confusion.

I went back to give Melody and Wellington 'leads', which resulted in successful, if pawky, jumps. Kingston, homing in like an angry meteorite, joined us on the far side of the fence. The operation was rather like one of those Christmas cracker puzzles where a farmer has a fox, a goose and a bag of corn and has to ferry them across a river without allowing their mutual destruction.

Although on our way again, things had become unsettled. Nicky was blaming John for Melody's refusal, John was telling Nicky to stop whingeing and sort her own horse out, and Pamela and Kingston were orbiting us like a sheepdog on speed as the former tried valiantly to remain in the same county as her team mates. This combination of altercation and orbiting played havoc with the team formation and, while I was still safely out in front, the others were taking fences − or not − in some disarray.

We came to the optional hedge, and I sailed over it. Behind, Nicky had determined to take a more balanced view of Wellington's abilities. 'We're not jumping that (fishwife's epithet) hedge', she declared loudly, and there was communal grinding to a halt (tangenital veering in Pamela's case), followed by further altercation and much barging in the muddy gateway.

Regrouping like some game remnant of the Light Brigade, we set off once again. The next fence was a concrete sewer pipe set in a ditch, and I had to give even my horse a slap and a kick into it. Behind me, John was beginning to enjoy himself. He secretly enjoyed arguing with Nicky and was probably also drifting into one of his highly coloured day-dreams, in which he became a Colonel in the Bengal Lancers, or Master of the Quorn. His enjoyment was heightened by the fact that the excitement and mayhem had geed up Melody, who was beginning to take hold of her bit and stride out in impressive style.

At the pipe-in-a-ditch stood a photographer, which was all the incentive John needed. Seeing visions of himself as centrefold in *Horse and Hound,* he crouched up over Melody's withers and let her surge on towards the jump. Her stop was a triumph of biomechanics. John performed a mighty back somersault and landed with a great thud across the sewer pipe.

Against my baser instincts, I pulled up and trotted back. John was still draped across the pipe, while the others looked down at him. Even Nicky seemed slightly concerned. The macho victim of many rugger scrums, still in Bengal

Lancer mode, twitched at the extremities and groaned 'I'm all right, you go on'. 'Okay', we said, and set off once more. But somehow, our hearts were no longer in it. Perhaps, beneath deep layers of callousness, there lurked a thin veneer of compassion. By some unspoken consensus, we pulled up after a couple more fences, and returned to the ditch, where John was being reassembled by a motherly first-aid lady. 'Are you sure you're all right,' we mumbled sheepishly. 'You rotten bastards' croaked John 'When I said go on, I didn't think you really would'.

What we didn't know at the time was that Sara's sister had videoed our round. Played fast backwards, the video formed the main attraction at the club's Christmas Social. The opening seconds showed John performing an amazing back flip out of nowhere, sailing over his horse's head and landing neatly in the saddle. John, his bodywork repaired, was at pains to point out the blend of aesthetics and athleticism, and dreamt of a career in the circus. Myself, I think he was attracted to the prospect of wearing spangly tights.

Riding Weekend

When I was a member of the Greater London Council Staff Riding Club we, in common with other staff clubs, received a subvention from the Council, and were in the fortunate position of being able to subsidise various activities. One activity mooted was a club trip to Dartmoor and, as it happened, most of those interested in the trip wished to go hunting. However, this was during the GLC's last years, when there was a left-wing administration, and it was perceived by the committee that the powers-that-were might take a dim view of subsidising staff participation in this activity, so it was agreed to advertise the trip simply as a 'riding weekend'. Since one of my functions within the club was to write reports on various events, it was suggested that I minimise any specific reference to h--t--g. This was the result:

Six personnel a-riding went
Betwixt the Darmoor bogs
And — purely by coincidence —
They met a pack of dogs.

One dog went 'woof' at Patrick's horse —
The horse took off in fright
And galloped straight across the moor
With Patrick clinging tight.

The others sniggered at his plight
And settled down to watch
Then, suddenly, they realised
That Patrick had the scotch.

Aghast, they galloped after him
Down valley and up tor
Quite heedless of the streams and rocks
They flew across the moor.

With terror upmost in their minds
And rescue as their task
Lest Patrick fall into a bog
And sink, complete with flask.

The miles and hours flashed, endless, by
They never slackened pace
They leapt stone walls and gates and sheep
And lovers, in their race.

At last they caught him near Haytor,
Flaked out, among the rocks
An empty hipflask in his hand
Beside him, one drunk fox.

Some local people in red coats
Rode up with hearty cheers
And said it was the longest run
They'd known for thirty years.

Now Patrick's famous — feted for
His legendary ride
His head and chest have swollen up
With most unseemly pride

But all his friends are unimpressed
In fact, they wish he'd burst
Their only memory of the day
Is one of unquenched thirst.

(In fairness to Patrick, it should be said that there are elements of poetic licence in these verses. However, he was 'riding' an ex-hurdler, and he did have a busy day. The lesson to be learnt from this — albeit somewhat apocryphal — tale, is never venture out on Dartmoor without a large, full hipflask. Apart from the primary application, it allows the possibility that other riders might interrupt a good run to rescue the flask, whereas they would be most unlikely to concern themselves with an unadorned colleague.)

HUNTING IN THE WEST COUNTRY

THERE IS STILL A POPULAR MISCONCEPTION that the chief concerns of anyone going hunting are whether they will be sent home for having the wrong sort of buttons on their coat and whether, when it comes to the crunch (unhappy phrase) they will be able to tackle a five-foot hedge with ditch and drop.

In the West Country, such considerations are totally irrelevant. Firstly, a significant number of the field do not have any buttons on their coats (especially after energetic pre-hunt liaisons in their horse boxes) and secondly, there are no five-foot hedges. It is true that, on the south western edge of Dartmoor, one could face a two hundred foot drop into a china clay quarry but, if one were sufficiently out of control to allow this, one would have long since fallen victim to the rocks, bogs, gorse, rifle ranges and savage local sheep.

No, the concerns of those hunting in the West Country are not those addressed in books on dress and etiquette nor yet those of city-slicker fashion victims descending upon the Shires. In this part of the world, things are more basic.

The first concern of a hunting day is that one should do justice to a farmhouse breakfast. If one is to spend five or six hours on Dartmoor or Exmoor, a good deal of fuel is called for. Provided that breakfast is taken early, and one resists the temptation to become flustered trying to tie a stock correctly, it is possible to spend a comatose half hour digesting grapefruit, muesli, bacon, eggs, sausages, fried bread, tea and toast much like a rock python dealing with a water

THE UP-COUNTRY MEET.

buffalo it has swallowed sideways. With practise, it is even possible to take such a meal on board and still find room for a spare hunt breakfast, if attending one of those highly civilised meets where such are on the agenda. The hunt breakfast, an institution on Dartmoor, is an excuse to huddle in the smoky warmth of a moorland inn, drinking copious amounts of whisky, watching and re-watching videos of the Field Master falling headfirst into a quagmire, bragging about past runs on half-crazed, hard-pulling horses and consuming more bacon, eggs, sausages and fried bread. The foregoing being such an attractive combination, a hunt breakfast usually disperses only when the whippers-in have been employed to chivvy the field out of the pub and into their saddles.

The second concern of hunting in the West Country lies in deciding what to wear. In saying this, I am not returning to questions of box-calf boots and swallow-tail coats. Indeed, in this part of the world, the locals laugh at you if you *do not* wear rubber boots and, once you've forded a few streams of uncertain depth and run alongside your horse through some 'wetlands' (junior bogs), you'll know why. Furthermore, many of the locals — including some well known Masters — wear hunt coats made of synthetic waterproof material: I, too, have one of these and although it makes me look like a mounted refuse sack there is nothing novel in this, and I have often been grateful for it.

No, the question of what to wear does not involve the outer garments; it is the number of layers beneath which is at issue. Logical reference to weather forecasts is of no help here. Forecasts — usually wrong anyway — have no chance of success in the West Country unless they read 'Occasional heatwaves interspersed with sleet, hail, driving rain and dense mist, with changes expected after lunch.' Even if one accepts that such a forecast might be half right, one is led back to the question of how to dress for it. The problem is further compounded by the fact that one is faced not only by changes in external conditions, but also by changes in one's own physical state occasioned by alternating flat

THE WEST COUNTRY MEET.

out gallops with periods of sitting stock still on exposed hillsides. Inevitably, the galloping coincides with periods of hot sunshine, while standing around heralds the arrival of rain driven by the sort of wind that threatens to disembowel you. Sitting on Exmoor above Porlock one February, I gained an almost mystical insight into how Captain Oates must have felt.

Not surprisingly, therefore, the question of what to wear transcends other pre-hunt worries such as what will the hired horse be like, and people spend the morning either sneaking furtive glances at each others layers or indulging in soul-searching debate: 'Last time I wore a tee shirt under my hunt shirt and my black/green/thick/thin sweater but it looks too hot/cold for that and I see you're wearing three thermal vests/a bikini so what do you think I should do?' If one is not careful, what should be the post-breakfast torpor can be destroyed by repeated trips to the bedroom to add or subtract garments, each visit being complicated by increasingly flustered stock-tying. To make a final decision, take a deep breath and walk to the car in what one is wearing at the time is, in its own way, an act of heroism.

The aforementioned worry about the hired horse is, in this part of the world, usually a waste of time. I have hired all sorts, shapes and sizes of West Country hunter, and they have varied from adequate to excellent (the adequate ones having been hired from the poshest yards). There has, of course, been the occasional interesting mount, most notably the notorious No Brakes Bill, who helped me discover in myself unkown sources of strength and stamina fuelled, no doubt, by two extremely large breakfasts. (No Brakes Bill was apportioned to me with the sort of back-handed compliment so prevalent in riding; 'We couldn't give him to anyone else' and, since the hirers had previously allowed me to enjoy several excellent days on their daughter's point-to-pointers, there was no ducking the issue: even mounted refuse sacks have their pride.)

However, No Brakes Bill aside, the West Country hunter is unlikely to prove problematical, and certain to prove surefooted (the fact that he is still standing up and breathing being evidence of the latter). One can, therefore, concentrate one's anxieties on more pressing questions: will it be safe to get off for a pee, will there be the opportunity to eat anything and will it be possible to drink more from other peoples' hipflasks than they drink from yours.

The first of these considerations is not, of course, confined to the West Country; it is equally embarrassing in any part of the world to be hoicked out of the bushes, as it were in midstream, by a horse who has just heard 'Gone away'. However, although the West Country does possess some suitable 'watering holes', it also contains great tracts of barren moorland and it is inevitably whilst traversing these that one hears the call. This being so, by the time some vaguely convenient rocks or bushes appear, the tendency is to throw caution, quite literally, to the winds. Although, for gentleman riders, the dangers of peeing into the wind are well known, it may only be experience which teaches that, downwind, it is possible to christen casually discarded gloves and whip from a remarkable distance. Furthermore, a wind that will carry the contents of one's bladder so effectively will do even more for the voice, and great care should be taken if, indulging in a communal leak, one opines upon the physical attributes of the girl on the chestnut, or upon the Master's idiosyncratic venery.

Given the previous emphasis upon breakfast, talk of the opportunity for eating might seem indulgent − even greedy. However, by three o'clock, even the most guar-gantuan breakfast(s) can be a faded memory, and I have known a grown man virtually whimper upon dropping his Mars bar into a muddy puddle. Since the act of removing clingfilm from a sandwich is as sure a way of encouraging hounds to 'find' as getting off to pee, talk of the *opportunity* to eat is something of a misnomer. The best thing to do is carry something concentrated and sustaining, such as a pork pie, which can be unwrapped one-handed and crammed into the mouth in mid-gallop. While I acknowledge that any form of riding-related bragging is usually ill-founded, and a prime way of tempting fate, I have to confess that I am extremely good at this manoeuvre, and have often provoked what I believe to have been open-mouthed looks of admiration from the cream of West Country hunting folk. The secret is to give the horse plenty of rein, and assist the pie from its wrapping with a Gelleresque concentration of willpower.

The hipflask question is undoubtedly the most difficult to deal with. If it were simply a matter of trading swigs with one's friends, there would obviously be an incentive to drink deeply from their flasks whilst shielding your own. I used to improve my chances in this respect by being the only one of my circle whose flask did not have a captive top, and pleading difficulty in keeping my horse still while using both hands to open it. Unfortunately, since witnessing my pie-eating skills, none of my friends swallow this ploy any more, and I have resorted to the craven device of skulking behind a rock for a quick swig. However, although this practice will serve amongst friends, it can appear churlish to strangers. One of the delights of hunting in the West Country is the friendliness of the locals, and one can hardly respond to a hunt member's invitation to 'come back afterwards for a drink or two' by disappearing into the foothills of the nearest tor. Furthermore, proffering a flask is a wonderful way of breaking the ice with attractive members of the opposite sex and, since these are many and thirsty down west, a flask tends to be quickly depleted. In principle, one could undertake an early sacrifice on one's own flask in such worthy causes, and then fling oneself on the mercy of one's friends, but this would doubtless provoke ribald and cynical comment, and thus take the edge off the day.

Flask management must, therefore, remain an opportunist guerilla procedure, which will occupy one's mental processes until the Master finally blows for home. When this happens, the last concern of the day is to accomplish the seven mile 'hack' back to the boxes with an air of 'is it over already?' disappointment, and not to give the impression of being on the verge of expiring from a combination of exhaustion, dehydration and alcohol poisoning. The first two will, in any case, be remedied by the West Country thermos concoction of hot water, honey and brandy, and one can then proceed to build up an immunity to the third by dining in the pub, where it is accepted etiquette to fall asleep in one's soup.

The Hunt Ball

The hotel venue sounds so posh
That we polish up our wellies
Our eyes are on the kitchen clock
Our minds are on our bellies.
We hurry off, all groomed and suave
(Though with bow ties askew)
Our tickets on hire purchase
But our underwear brand new.
After frantic navigation
The hotel is run to ground
Then we hang about the foyer
Trying not to buy a round
And the place is full of strangers —
People who we're never seen
All in dinner suits and ballgowns
All coiffured, polite and clean
And we look round for our hunting friends
Who we will recognise
By their mud-besplattered faces
And their whisky-reddened eyes.
We keep listening for their curses
Look for rough, unshaven cheeks
But we still can't see those women
We've been hunting with for weeks.
Then, at last, vague recognition
Joyous shock and disbelief;
The mud and blood washed off

Revealing beauty underneath.
Then amazement's interrupted
As the dinner horn resounds
And the congregation pours in
Like a pack of eager hounds —
But check beside the table plan
And back and forth they cast
Fearing that they've been omitted
And will have to stand and fast
There is gloom and consternation
But at last all find their places
And with matchless hybrid vigour
They begin to fill their faces
There is elbowing and munching
Unremitting 'til, twixt courses
They chat up each other's spouses
And tell lies about their horses.
Then, at last, the meal is finished —
All have done their very best
And they lean back as the Chairman
Stands to introduce the guest.
As he tells his hoary tales
The distraction comes in handy
One effects intense attention
And drinks someone else's brandy.
And, when the guest is finished
It's the Master's turn to rise
Exhorting us 'hunt twice a week —
Get vastly muscled thighs'
But by surreptitious glances
(Trying not to seem perverted)
We confirm our shrewd suspicion
He's addressing the converted.
And with the speeches over
And the floor prepared for dancing
There is barging, there is bumping
Pirouettes, piaffe and prancing
There is whinnying and nipping

And, of cleavage, the odd faceful
Conduct which, within the field
Would be censured as disgraceful
And then, just as one is hoping
Things will get severely rude,
We are foiled in our efforts
By the raffle interlude.
As is normal with such ventures
There are many cries of 'fix'
For the Master wins four prizes
And the Chairman's wife wins six
While the kennel huntsman's daughter
Who's bought tickets by the score
Remains quite unrewarded —
As the Master wins yet more
She stays tense with expectation
Till at last the draw's completed
And we hasten to console her
As she cries that she's been cheated
Perhaps the raffle organiser
Will be run clean out of town —
But then the band strikes up again,
The lights, once more, go down
And one learns, in close-clinched boogie
That an all-devouring kiss
From the kennel huntsman's daughter
Is the pinnacle of bliss.

OF HUMAN BONDAGE

CAPTAIN RONNIE WALLACE MFH IS PROBABLY the most eminent figure in contempary hunting circles so, when his biography was published, it was no surprise that *Horse and Hound* ran a feature on it. This made much of the Captain's time as Master of the Heythrop and of his 'sending home' of many and various well-connected miscreants. Reading this with some relish, I was reminded of a day out with the Exmoor, of which the Captain has been Master in recent years.

It was a good day and us visitors were, typically, made welcome by everyone connected with the hunt. Much of this welcome was sealed by the interchanging of neat spirits and, by mid-afternoon, these had permeated to Pamela's extremities, turning her exceptionally pink and giggly. Now Pamela has an unconstrained comic imagination and a hunting whip with a very long lash, and Exmoor hospitality proved to be the catalyst which triggered their interaction. Applying some nimble knotwork to the lash, she manoeuvred her horse next to mine and neatly lassoed me.

Overcome with triumph and racked with barely suppressed mirth, she kept a tight hold as I tried in vain to extricate myself without attracting the attention of Captain Wallace, who I happened to be following at a distance of about ten feet. Fortunately Pamela, who was absolutely cracking up, found herself with a choice between letting go or laughing herself out of her own saddle and, rather surprisingly, chose the former course. I never discovered,

OF HUMAN BONDAGE.

therefore, whether being a bondage victim was a sending home offence. I always doubted that Pamela would have been in danger of ignominious dismissal; knowing hunting people as I do, I guess that such behaviour on the part of a lady would be actively encouraged, possibly by the offer of a reduced subscription.

OF EQUINE BANDAGE.

QUALIFYING

I AM ONE OF THOSE APPARENTLY RARE, strange people who
think it is a privilege to help qualify point-to-pointers, and
an honour to be asked to do so. For those unfamiliar with
the term, qualifying consists of getting a horse through eight
half days behind hounds without doing him terminal damage,
and without oneself being irrevocably ostracised by those
members of the field who are actually trying to hunt.

As with most equestrian pursuits, qualifying tends
to be less glamorous than it may at first seem, and attempts
to qualify often amount simply to driving fifty miles at the
break of dawn, to discover that the horse has colic or the
meet has been lost to fog. Also, horses being horses, if one
does get to ride, there is more chance of being the victim of
ignominy than of displaying skill, dash, boldness, gallantry
or any of the other virtues mythically associated with gentlemen on blood horses.

This point is amply illustrated by what befell me at the
end of a relatively innocous day when my friend Simon and
I took his two horses out with the Chiddingfold, Leconfield
and Cowdray. With the ground frozen and snow falling
steadily, much time had been spent skulking hopefully in the
shelter of some woodland. Simon's horses, rather fitter than
most of the other qualifiers, had been entertaining the field
in its pedestrian progress by playfully pirouetting and trying
to climb trees and when — for some obscure reason — we
did get an opportunity for a gallop, Simon's mount, Bumble,
exhibited sufficient zest for us to become separated. I, there-

fore, arrived back at the box first, loaded my horse, and took grateful recourse to my hipflask.

When Simon returned, I went to help him rug up and load the inherently clumsy, bargy Bumble, who was still exhibiting symptoms of equine St. Vitus' dance. Somehow, the catches on the ramp had become stuck and, with Simon doing technical things from the inside, I ill-advisedly tried to assist with one hand, while holding Bumble's reins with the other. Even more ill-advisedly, I tried to perform this task while standing atop a conical mound of frozen earth in my leather-soled boots.

Simon and I had just become fully absorbed in an advanced ramp-freeing technique known as synchronised swearing when another horse box rattled past the corner of ours. On seeing this out of the corner of one eye Bumble, true to character, half-reared and whipped round. Instinctively, I tried to hang on to the reins but, my footing being so precarious, I was unceremoniously whisked off the mound and flew through the air at great speed, landing on my back in the snow and banging my head on the frozen ground.

Having exorcised his neurosis, Bumble trotted off up the road, to be neatly fielded by a well known lady race-rider. At first, thinking that I was the victim of some intrepid, but heroically failed endeavour, she and her colleagues gathered round to express concern but, when I explained what had happened, they began to murmer 'Oh, I see', and edge away. It must be said that this was still a much kinder response than I had expected.

At the time, I assumed that lady point-to-pointers from Sussex must be very well brought up. However, having subsequently seen photographs of a local Hunt Ball, I now know that this is not the case, and therefore conclude that their faces were simply too numb for them to guffaw properly.

'THE ONLY THING HE'LL QUALIFY FOR IS A FREE BUS PASS.'

Racegoing

Look out the thermal underwear, pull on the thermal socks
And several sweaters and the old waxed coat
'Cos it's raining down at Fontwell — it's been pouring there all week
So we'd better pick some horses who can float.
Seek out the fur-lined wellies, and the brolly and a hat
And be sure to fill the hipflask to the brim
'Cos it's raining down at Fontwell — they'll need lifeboats in the
    straight —
If you see one wearing waterwings, back him.

No, I don't like Royal Ascot with the wallies in top hats
And all the blue-blood horses owned by sheiks
Just take me down to Fontwell with its rain and mud and mist
And selling-chasers with no brains or brakes.
Yes, I'd rather share pork pies with some ruddy cheeked old guys
Watching horses doing breaststroke through the mire
Than sip illicit champers nicked from Fortnum's dearest hampers
Bought by chinless toffs in Savile Row attire.

Pull out the final fiver, there's a chaser in the last
Who is often given time faults, he's so slow
But although he's none too fleet, I've been told he's got webbed feet
And we'll toast him in the bar before we go.

The Jockeys' Prayer

Jockeys are small and pious men
With knees beneath their chins
They ride in attitudes of prayer
As if confessing sins
And, poised in constant genuflection,
They plead for Heavenly protection:

'Lord, we consort with stable girls
And cheat the Clerk of Scales
And we get odds-on favourites stuck
Securely on the rails.
We know, at times, such human flaws
Transgress Divine or temporal laws
But, howsoe'er Thy judgement serve us,
From zealous stewards, Lord, preserve us'.

Paranoia

Judge not, that ye be not judged
A maxim I've neglected
One rider leaves the ring, all smiles,
The others scowl, rejected.
One thinks me most astute and wise
A paragon of judges
The rest all think me thick or blind
And slink off, bearing grudges.
The ringside pundits shake their heads —
Their own dissents forgotten
There's long and loud consensus that
The judge was truly rotten.

JUDGING

It is not until one has been 'invited' to judge that one realises how cruelly efficient was the old Indian potentate's ploy of giving a white elephant to someone who had incurred his displeasure. The idea behind this was that, since the white elephant was such a rare and revered creature, the recipient could not refuse the gift without giving great insult but, in attempting to keep it in the requisite degree of luxury, he would rapidly go broke.

Being 'invited' to judge is the modern equivalent. The 'invitation' is so absurdly flattering that it appears churlish (and perhaps self-deprecating) to refuse, but acceptance brings its own waking nightmare; a Pandora's box of Pony Club mums, forgotten dressage tests ('It wasn't an error of course, it was an error of judgement') unobserved curbs and spavins, unnoticed exhibitors and tirades from hatchet-faced women (or worse, chinless and pedantic men) along the lines of 'I was placed *third* by Delia Ffarting-Smythe last week, and *she judges* at *county* level'. (To which one cannot readily reply, as one would wish, 'If the crazed old bat likes horses so fat they can hardly waddle across the ring, that's her problem'.)

There may, of course, be a measure of difference between the Indian potentate's gift and the show organiser's 'invitation'; whereas the former's intent was undoubtedly malicious, the latter's only *might* be. She (it is always a lady) *may* have been put down the line by you at another show and be seeking revenge ('I'll inveigle him up to our show so that my friends can see what a useless, incompetent, dithering apology for a judge he really is') but, on the other hand, she may simply be desperate. Such desperation can, if not adequately disguised, rather take the gilt off the flattery of the 'invitation'. This is more likely to become apparent if you cannot make the show date and start – helpfully – to drop other judges of your acquaintance in it. By the time you have reeled off a list of people who you know 'would be delighted to help out' only to be told a dozen times 'I've already tried him/her', it begins to dawn on you that you were not, in fact, first choice. Furthermore, it will probably also become apparent that, in addition to not knowing you from Adam, the organiser only got your name and number from her eleventh choice, who gave it out of revenge for your having drunk the entire contents of his hipflask last time you hunted together.

Of course, if you *can* make the date, such ignominious truths will remain buried. You will be told what a wonderful person you are, and how thrilled they are you can come, and the organiser will go to bed exhausted, thinking 'I hope he turns up/on the right day/can recognise a horse in a field of sheep/doesn't want more than a fiver in expenses.'

On the morning of the show, you can absolutely guarantee that it will be either insufferably hot and humid, or else freezing cold and raining fit to presage a second Flood. The ground will be either iron hard and rutted, or fetlock deep in glutinous mud, making it virtually impossible to spot unlevelness in any horse who still possesses an even number of legs.

Arriving at the show ground, you will seek to slink in as unobtrusively as possible, trying to avoid confidence-denting comments from early arrivals: 'Oh heavens, he's not judging is he – I'm going to ask for my entry fees back'. In similarly low-key mode, you will then try to seek out somebody in authority. This is usually not easy, partly because the person who originally approached you will not be at the show. People on show committees necessarily have finely honed instincts of self-preservation, and there is a tacit understanding that, having *organised* judges, there is no point in being around to carry the can if they fail to appear, or cause such chaos that non-appearance would have been preferable. One's tentative 'Good morning, is _____ around?' will, therefore, receive several puzzled responses from the-man-putting-up-the-toilets and some early morning dog walkers before, eventually, one meets somebody who is at least on the periphery of the organisation. Having established that _____ is not around because she had a row with her boy-friend last night and has gone back to her parents – or whatever is the shorthand of the day for 'I've done my bit booking the judges and I'm buggered if I'm going to stand in a wet field all day getting pneumonia' – one can announce the reason for one's presence, and hope that 'Ah, well, she asked me to judge classes two and three' will not be met by an imperfectly suppressed snort of disbelief followed by the asphyxiated chicken noise people make when a thin veneer of politeness prevents them from actually rolling around on

'ALL THE KING'S HORSES AND ALL THE KING'S MEN NEEDED

the ground plucking tufts of grass and bellowing with unconstrained laughter.

When I first met my friend Anita, her response to my announcing myself was to summon a minion and say, imperiously, 'This is a judge. Take it away, feed it, give it a drink, and tell it what to do'. For the uninitiated, I should explain that this, to a judge, represents warm welcome. Once the initial glow of self-importance has been dispersed by the cold realisation that one has actually got to get out there and perform, being fed and watered becomes, like the condemned man's last breakfast, the only satisfying reality. Indeed, I can recall the time when a fellow judge became so satisfactorily fed and watered that he could hardly stand or talk, which left me as a last minute substitute to judge the working hunter class. As it happened, rather than being a burden, this gave me a welcome excuse to decline the show organiser's suggestion that I ride her horse in the class; a flattering idea, but one that could have provoked

OVER THERE, MR. DIGGLE.'

accusations of incest and nepotism unacceptable even by showing standards.

Just as a condemned man takes comfort from a priest, so a judge will take comfort from his essential ally, the ring steward (or, if judging dressage, the writer). The type of people who volunteer for such tasks are, without doubt, the salt of the earth. They will give up a perfectly good Sunday to stand or sit, anonymous and often perplexed, while the judge beside them alternates between spouting sotto voce jargon from the corner of his mouth and indulging in embarrassing periods of agonised self-doubt.

Ring stewards and writers tend to divide into two types: the weather-beaten, highly competent type who could quite easily manage single-handed were you to sneak off to the loo or beer tent, and the novicy, but desperate-to-learn-and-please type, who idolise you without realising that you not only have feet of clay, but that you degenerate from there upward. Which is the more comforting of the two depends largely upon circumstance: if you are suffering serious harassment from a galleon shaped Pony Club mum, the former is likely to sail to your aid like a beak-prowed trireme, muttering the ring steward equivalent of 'Go ahead, punk, make my day'. If, on the other hand, a class has gone surprisingly well, and you have sent the placed exhibitors off on a lap of honour without the usual gut-wrenching pangs of guilt, then the latter's hero worshipping offer to fetch tea and cake will be more welcome than the former's brittle 'Did you notice the pasterns on that grey you placed third?'

I once surprised a dressage competitor who was preparing to halt at X by beating my writer about the head with a rolled up schedule. I was not, however, expressing dissatisfaction with her performance, but simply trying to protect her from the ravages of a horsefly, one of whose cousins had previously caused a riderless horse to proceed across the arena from A to M in extended bolt. This was the only occasion on which I have struck an assistant, although the one time I unwisely used a friend (John Cherrington) as a ring steward, I could readily have throttled him.

After a good lunch, I took advantage of our friendship to relax, and couched my opinions of the exhibits and their riders in South London idiom rather than the usual diplomatic judgespeak. John helpfully recorded all these observations verbatim, and I subsequently had to display considerable mental and physical agility to find reason and opportunity to retrieve the comments sheet before it found its way to the secretary's tent.

In normal circumstances, I like to make notes when judging. Especially with a bigger class, notes help recall points which might otherwise be overlooked if one tried to keep all one's impressions in one's head. They can also be of value in helping to pre-empt the (tacit or overt) 'Why am I placed here?' queries which spring to the minds, if not lips, of every exhibitor who has not won or, indeed, has been placed below 'that fat woman with bad hands on the common cob' (a description applicable to virtually any combination which has been placed above you in any showing class). In my experience, it is usually mollifying for an exhibitor to have a judge *volunteer* a reason for his placing; even if they do not agree with it, at least it suggests that the judge remembers and recognises them, and did not pick the placed horses at random and in panic after an hour-long charade. There is, indeed, a breed of exhibitor who tends to have more respect for a judge who has noticed a defect and placed them down, than one who has failed to notice it at all. It goes without saying, however, that any such defect has to be genuine and relevant, and that one should not make recourse to Cherrington-inspired notes and say 'I would have placed you second, but the girl on the bay's got a nicer bum than yours'. For the aspiring judge, the correct way of expressing this sentiment is 'I liked yours almost as much, but number 33 is slightly more impressive behind'. But they won't tell you that on a judges' course.

Dressage Dialogue: A Judge Explains His Marking

'Oh, it's really a pest when you're riding a test
On a horse who won't stop then won't budge
To be watched with sour gaze and then damned with faint praise
By a truly inept looking judge.

Now I've just seen my score and the highest mark's four
And I note that you've given a one
So I hope, in due course, you'll get up on my horse
And we'll see just how things should be done'.

'Though your offer is kind it is sadly declined —
I would love to put him through his paces
But at this time and place I'd risk public disgrace
For my breeches are split in key places.

I am moved, nonetheless, by your patent distress
To provide step-by-step explanation
As to how I assessed what I'd sum up, if pressed,
As a setback for true equitation.

Well, you entered at A in the usual way
Then rode ten pirouettes out of bolt
Then his blatant reaction to sexual distraction
Confirmed that your mount is a colt.

When he tried to have sex somewhere north-east of X
With a cob mare both plain and unchaste
I admired his impulsion but felt great revulsion
At such aberration of taste.

'EXCELLENT ENGAGEMENT, WEIGHT WELL PLACED ON
HINDQUARTERS, GOOD ELEVATION AND RHYTHM . . . 10.'

125

And despite great self-carriage, his efforts at marriage
Involved you in error of course;
Though engagement is great the term does not relate
To a coupling with some other horse.

Your eventual frustration of his assignation
Caused more loss of marks — I should mention
That his grinding his teeth and the noise from his sheath
Are both classical symptoms of tension.

It's not merely as if one could just call him stiff —
With his heart and his mind still on mating
He remained so excited he went disunited
And Nemesis, clearly, was waiting.

As your half-pass began he immediately ran
All askew, to the site of his passion
Crossing legs in his state put the seal on his fate
In quite breath-taking, heart-stopping fashion.

So he stood, as one dead, Losgelassenheit fled
A sad picture of anguish and shock
And, but for one wheeze and his trembling knees,
He could well have been fashioned from rock.

So I felt great distaste at your untimely haste
When you tried to continue the test
And your out-of-breath steed plaited weakly, knock-kneed
Wanting only to lie down and rest.

It's apparent, in fact, that your riding lacks tact;
Your coercion, untempered by skill
Makes viewing less pleasant than watching some peasant
Push cartloads of dung up a hill.

Since your talent's so small you should not ride at all,
But a colt of such presence and size
Quite upstanding and grand, should be shown off in hand
Where he'd have every chance of first prize.'

The Last Word

At ninety, in his rocking chair,
Urged on to reminisce
The horseman's mind flew down the years
And what he said was this:

'Oh, I have crashed through countless gates
And nosedived many ditches
And learnt adrenalin is brown
Behind the Fernie bitches.

And I have scattered many poles
And missed a million strides
And fallen off in point-to-points
On nearly all my rides.

And I've done dressage at the charge —
Whole tests performed in bolt
Once, judging the 'best filly foal'
I placed a lusty colt.

There have been mounts I could not start
And mounts I could not stop
But I took pride in every ride
When I remained on top.

For those of us who go astride
Find triumph in small measure
Each hour of dignity preserved
Is valued beyond treasure.

And anyone who rides to brag
Is riding for a fall
A horse can make far greater yet
The greatest fool of all.

Yet there's one thing I dare to boast
That no-one can begrudge
For all my faults I never was
A Prix Caprilli judge.'